**NEW ORLEANS
SAINTS**

JULIE NELSON

Published by Creative Education
123 South Broad Street, Mankato, Minnesota 56001
Creative Education is an imprint of The Creative Company

Designed by Rita Marshall

Photos by: Allsport USA, AP/Wide World Photos, Bettmann/CORBIS,
SportsChrome

Library of Congress Cataloging-in-Publication Data

Nelson, Julie.
New Orleans Saints / by Julie Nelson.
p. cm. — (NFL today)
Summary: Traces the history of the New Orleans Saints from the team's
beginnings through 1999.
ISBN 1-58341-051-1

1. New Orleans Saints (Football team)—History—Juvenile literature.
[1. New Orleans Saints (Football team)—History. 2. Football—History.]
I. Title. II. Series: NFL today (Mankato, Minn.)

GV956.N366N45   2000
796.332'64'0976335—dc21   99-023745

9 8 7 6 5 4 3 2

New Orleans, Louisiana, is a city famous for its food, fun, and French heritage. Every year, thousands of tourists flock to the city to celebrate its winter Mardi Gras festival or to take in an evening of jazz at one of the famous Bourbon Street nightclubs. Because of its role in the development of this unique musical style, New Orleans is often called "the birthplace of jazz."

In 1967, New Orleans also became the birthplace of a new National Football League franchise—the Saints. The team quickly won the hearts of New Orleans sports fans. Over time, it would break a lot of hearts as well with its in-

Saints quarterback legend Archie Manning.

ability to win consistently. It took the Saints 21 years to record their first winning season, despite the efforts of many talented and exciting players. Electrifying passer Archie Manning, hard-charging back George Rogers, and indestructible linebacker Rickey Jackson gave the New Orleans faithful some remarkable performances over the years, but wins never came easily.

1 9 6 7

Running back Jim Taylor led the first-year Saints in rushing with 390 yards.

THE SAINTS COME MARCHING IN

The saga of the Saints began on November 1, 1966, when NFL commissioner Pete Rozelle announced that New Orleans had been granted an NFL expansion franchise that would begin play the following season. Mayor Victor Schiro proudly told local citizens that New Orleans was now officially a "big-league" city.

John Mecom, a 29-year-old businessman and sports enthusiast from Houston, Texas, purchased the new football franchise for $8.5 million. He named the new club the Saints, after the famous jazz song that was so popular in New Orleans: "When the Saints Go Marchin' In."

Mecom, the league's youngest owner, liked to sit on the sidelines with his players. In fact, he didn't mind getting into the action now and then. When New Orleans played the New York Giants in 1967, several angry Giants players jumped Saints defensive end Doug Atkins after a play, knocking him to the ground. An indignant Mecom leaped off the bench and ran onto the field to try to stop the fight. New York player Freeman White swung at Mecom with his helmet, but the owner ducked and returned a punch that

Dominant pass rusher Wayne Martin.

Receiver Danny Abramowicz had a career season, catching 73 passes for 1,051 yards.

leveled White. The Saints would lose the game 21–27, but a fiery precedent had been set in New Orleans.

In 1967, Mecom hired Tom Fears to be the team's first head coach. As a player in the 1950s, Fears had been a fine receiver and a member of the 1951 Los Angeles Rams NFL championship team. As a coach, Fears had served as an assistant to Vince Lombardi, the legendary Green Bay Packers mentor. Fears was a tough, demanding coach. Players under his command complained that a Fears-led practice was "like a three-hour ride in a washing machine."

Like most expansion teams, the Saints were a curious mixture of aging veterans and untried rookies. Two such players were strong-armed quarterback Billy Kilmer, a seven-year pro picked up from the San Francisco 49ers, and wide receiver Danny Abramowicz, a rookie 17th-round draft pick from Ohio's Xavier University. Abramowicz would catch 50 passes from Kilmer, including six for touchdowns, during the 1967 season. The club's top runner its first season was Jim Taylor, a former Green Bay Packers All-Pro and future Hall-of-Famer.

The Saints got off to a slow start, losing their first seven games and finishing their inaugural season at 3–11. The next year, the club went 4–9–1. Although seven wins in two years was not what the Saints had hoped for, it was the best two-season total of any NFL expansion team to date.

In 1969, Abramowicz led the NFL in receptions with 73 and was named All-Pro. The Saints added another weapon that year, signing Tom Dempsey, a free agent placekicker. Dempsey had succeeded in football despite being born without a right hand and without toes on his right foot.

When he kicked, he wore a special snub-nosed shoe specially designed for him.

Dempsey experienced one of his greatest moments midway through the 1970 season. The Saints' 0–7 start had prompted Mecom to fire Tom Fears and replace him with J. D. Roberts. In Roberts's first game, New Orleans trailed Detroit 17–16 with the ball on their own 45-yard line and only seconds remaining. Roberts sent in Dempsey to attempt a 63-yard field goal.

Although the NFL record at the time was 56 yards, Dempsey was confident as he waited for the snap. As soon as holder Joe Scarpati put the ball down, Dempsey drilled it through the uprights, setting a long-distance record that would go unmatched for 18 years.

1 9 7 0

Tom Dempsey provided New Orleans' main highlight of the year—a 63-yard field goal.

A Good Manning Is Hard to Find

Saints fans hoped that Tom Dempsey's incredible kick would signal a new era of winning in the 1970s. Although that would not be the case, the new decade did bring a new star to the team—a flamboyant quarterback from Mississippi named Archie Manning.

Manning made his debut in the 1971 season opener against the Los Angeles Rams, a team the Saints had never beaten. Though regularly battered by fierce Rams defenders, Manning passed for one touchdown, then ran for another on the final play of the game to lead the Saints to a 24–20 upset win.

After several fine years, Manning sat out the 1976 season with severe tendinitis. After two operations and many long physical therapy sessions, he came back better than ever,

All-Pro Saints linebackers Rickey Jackson . . .

. . . and Pat Swilling.

*Running back
Tony Galbreath set
a team record with
146 rushing yards
in a single game.*

earning trips to the Pro Bowl in 1978 and '79. During those years, Manning became known as a great player stuck on a poor team. "I've always said Archie was a franchise player without a franchise," former Saints coach Hank Stram once said. "He'd be in the Hall of Fame if he'd had better players around him."

In his 12-year career (1971–82) with New Orleans, Manning set most of the club's passing records. He was more than just a great football player, though. He was also a much-admired citizen who devoted time to such causes as the Special Olympics and the Salvation Army. In 1978, Manning was honored with the Byron "Whizzer" White Award in recognition of contributions made to his team, community, and country.

A skilled ball thief, safety Tommy Myers.

During the last half of the 1970s, the Saints were led by two of football's most colorful coaches—Hank Stram (1976–77) and Dick Nolan (1978–80). Their job was to surround Manning with talent and to fill the nearly 70,000 seats of the huge Louisiana Superdome, which had opened before the 1975 season.

Young talent soon began to arrive. Chuck Muncie, an All-American running back from California, was Stram's top draft pick in 1976. He was joined by Tony Galbreath, an excellent runner and clutch receiver. The offensive combination of Manning, Muncie, Galbreath, and tight end Henry Childs—along with an improving defense featuring lineman Elois Grooms and safety Tommy Myers—helped the Saints edge toward their longstanding goal of a winning season.

Wes Chandler was New Orleans' top receiver, gaining 975 yards.

In 1978, under Nolan, the Saints came close. Manning threw for 3,416 yards and was named the Player of the Year in the National Football Conference. His pinpoint passing helped the Saints win five of their first nine games before a late season fade dropped their record to 7–9.

Finally, in 1979, New Orleans reached the .500 mark, finishing 8–8. Manning had another fine season, as did receiver Wes Chandler, who caught 65 passes for 1,069 yards. The big hero that year, however, was Muncie, who set club records with 1,198 rushing yards and 11 touchdowns and was named the Most Valuable Player in the Pro Bowl. Led by this talented trio, the Saints scored 370 points during the season—a new franchise record.

"We're going to be there very soon," linebacker Joe Federspiel told reporters. "This town is dying for a winner, and everyone on this team is dying to be one."

Quarterback Ken Stabler completed nearly 62 percent of his passes.

Unfortunately, "dying" is just what the Saints did in 1980. The club lost its first 14 games, and most of the scores weren't even close. The defense fell apart entirely, and the offense suffered after Muncie was traded to San Diego. By midseason, the media began referring to the team as the "Ain'ts." Clearly, it was time for a change.

The man brought in to oversee the change was former Houston Oilers coach O.A. "Bum" Phillips, who stalked the sidelines clad in lizard-skin cowboy boots, blue jeans, a plaid western shirt, and a Stetson hat. Like the Saints, the Oilers had been losers before Phillips arrived and turned the franchise around.

Phillips had built a powerful offense in Houston around Hall of Fame running back Earl Campbell, and he set out to construct a similar club in New Orleans. He used the number one pick in the 1981 NFL draft to acquire South Carolina running back George Rogers, the reigning Heisman Trophy winner as the best college player in the country. In his first year, Rogers led the league in rushing with 1,674 yards and 13 touchdowns, both new Saints records. His fine season also earned him a spot in the Pro Bowl and Offensive Rookie of the Year honors.

Phillips also drafted linebacker Rickey Jackson from Pittsburgh and tight end Hoby Brenner from Southern California in 1981. Both would star in New Orleans for the next 13 seasons. Jackson, who was quickly named defensive captain, would go on to set club records for games played (195) and quarterback sacks (123). Brenner became a fine blocker and

Rushing sensation George Rogers.

Courageous quarterback Archie Manning.

receiver. Over his career, he averaged more than 20 receptions and nearly 300 receiving yards per season.

Rogers and fullback Wayne Wilson gave the Saints solid offensive power in the backfield, but the club needed a quarterback. Age and injuries had finally taken their toll on Manning. Phillips convinced Ken Stabler, his former signal-caller in Houston, to join the Saints in 1982, bringing much-needed experience and leadership to the young team.

Two years later, Phillips brought another former Houston star, Earl Campbell, to New Orleans. Campbell was nearing the end of his outstanding NFL career, but Phillips was sure that the Hall-of-Famer had something left in his powerful legs. "Earl Campbell may not be in a class by himself," Phillips commented, "but whatever class he's in, it doesn't take long to call the roll."

The influx of new talent nearly put the Saints on the winning track. The team finished 4–5, 8–8, and 7–9 from 1982 to 1984, nearly making the playoffs each year. In fact, the Saints came within seconds of achieving their first winning season and earning a playoff spot in 1983. But a last-second field goal by Los Angeles Rams kicker Mike Lansford turned a 24–23 New Orleans lead into a 26–24 loss. Disappointed Saints fans wondered if things would ever change.

Morten Andersen set a new team scoring record with 120 total points.

WINNERS AT LAST

Big changes began taking place in New Orleans in 1985. A 5–11 record that year led to Bum Phillips's departure, Earl Campbell's retirement, and a trade that sent George Rogers to the Washington Redskins. All of this came on the

Hard-hitting defense is a Saints trademark (pages 18-19).

*Halfback Rueben
Mayes was the
NFL's top rookie
rusher, gaining
1,353 yards.*

heels of the team's sale in May 1985 to New Orleans businessman Tom Benson.

Benson had some definite goals in mind when he took over the club. "There is a difference between wanting to win and having to win," he said. "In our case, we have to win. We have to put in extra effort that leads to achievement. When you have to win, you really look for the extra things that can make you successful."

One of those extra "things" was Jim Finks, who was named president and general manager of the Saints in 1986. With a 37-year career in sports, Finks offered New Orleans the steady guidance that the team needed. Finks's first move was to hire Jim Mora as head coach. Mora had been the top coach of the United States Football League, a league that lasted only a few seasons in the 1980s.

Mora's first season in New Orleans turned out to be a difficult transition for both the players and the coach. The team got off to a dismal 1–4 start, and Mora fined, benched, and even cut players until he found a winning combination. The club then made a turnaround in midseason, winning five of six games, and finished the season with a 7–9 record—a big improvement over 1985, but still below what Mora expected of himself and his team.

Still, the Saints' offense was clearly on the rise. Rookie running backs Rueben Mayes and Dalton Hilliard had proven to be solid draft picks, and Dave Wilson and former USFL star Bobby Hebert, a Louisiana native, shared the quarterbacking duties effectively. Mora had also concentrated on building a strong offensive line to protect his quarterback and open up holes for his fast young running backs. The keys to his newly built line were center Joel Hilgenberg, guard Brad Edelman, and tackle Stan Brock.

The defense was also beginning to solidify. Rickey Jackson, who earned a fourth consecutive Pro Bowl berth in 1986, was joined at linebacker by Pat Swilling, a rookie, and Sam Mills, a former USFL standout under Mora. Together, they formed one of the top linebacker trios in the league.

The club had another budding star as well. Placekicker Morten Andersen was developing into one of the most accurate long-range field goal kickers in the league. A native of Denmark, Andersen had never kicked a football before coming to the United States as a 17-year-old exchange student. Once college coaches saw how well his soccer kicking style worked on a football, he was heavily recruited. Andersen

1 9 8 7

Linebacker Sam Mills anchored the Saints defense and earned his first Pro Bowl berth.

Eric Martin led New Orleans in receiving for seven seasons.

Innovative signal-caller Bobby Hebert.

chose to attend Michigan State University before the Saints selected him in the 1982 NFL draft.

These players were the nucleus of the New Orleans team playing its 21st season in the league in 1987. Before the year began, owner Tom Benson told reporters, "When you're 21, you become a man." His comment was a challenge to his players to become winners at last. They did just that.

The Saints opened the season with an impressive home win over Cleveland. Mayes shredded the Browns defense with 147 rushing yards, while the Saints defense set a franchise record with two safeties. New Orleans then moved to 3–3 before winning nine straight games to finish 12–3. Hebert threw for more than 2,000 yards, and Mayes and Hilliard combined for nearly 1,500 yards on the ground. Wide receiver Eric Martin also grabbed 44 passes for seven touchdowns. To no one's surprise, Jim Mora was named NFL Coach of the Year.

In their first-ever playoff game, the Saints faced the Minnesota Vikings in the Superdome on January 3, 1988. After the opening kickoff, New Orleans marched steadily down the field. A 10-yard scoring strike from Hebert to Martin capped off the drive and put the Saints up 7–0. Unfortunately, the hometown fans had little else to cheer about as the Vikings went on to win in a 44–10 rout.

The Saints kept winning in 1988, going 10–6 and barely missing a return to the playoffs. Over the next four years, the Saints enjoyed three more winning seasons—including a 12–4 campaign in 1992—and made the playoffs three straight years from 1990 to 1992. "We've come a long way since that first season," Mora said. "But it's not important

1 9 9 1

Under coach Jim Mora, the Saints started the year with a 7–0 record.

Michael Haynes used his blazing speed to collect a team-high 985 receiving yards.

where we've been at this point. It's where we're going. We want to be the best team in the NFL."

What happened next, however, seemed to defy explanation. Right when they seemed to be nearing the top of the NFL mountain in the early 1990s, the Saints began to fade back into the pack. In 1993, they dropped to 8–8 (after a 5–0 start), and in 1994 and 1995, the team fell below .500.

"I think there will be a lot of evaluations made and a lot of soul-searching done by everyone on the team," said offensive tackle Richard Cooper. "These have been the kinds of seasons you wake up thinking about . . . for a long time."

One explanation for the drop-off was injuries and changes in personnel, particularly on defense. In 1993, Pat Swilling departed as a free agent, and Sam Mills, defensive linemen

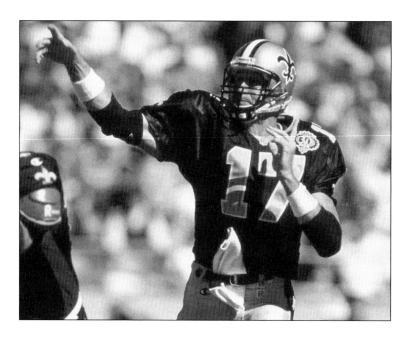

Record-setting quarterback Jim Everett.

Jim Wilks and Frank Warren, and defensive back Brett Maxie were hurt. Popular general manager Jim Finks also retired during the 1993 season because of illness. His death before the 1994 season dampened team spirits even further.

EVERETT EXPANDS EXPECTATIONS

1 9 9 6

Defensive tackle Wayne Martin led the club with 11 quarterback sacks.

True to his competitive nature, Jim Mora was unwilling to let the Saints just fade away. In 1994, he began rebuilding the team.

Keying the Saints' revival was quarterback Jim Everett, whose career had had its ups and downs. During his eight years with the Los Angeles Rams, Everett passed for more than 3,000 yards in five straight seasons—one of the most impressive streaks in the NFL. But he had also earned a reputation for being unable to win the big game. Mora disagreed. "In my opinion, Everett is one of the top quarterbacks in the league," Mora said. "He's got stats that are right up there with the best."

To support Everett, the Saints signed free agent wideout Michael Haynes. With Haynes added to receivers Quinn Early and Torrance Small and versatile tight end Irv Smith, New Orleans presented opposing defenses with one of the top passing attacks in the league.

This powerful offense clicked in 1994. Everett set club records with 346 completions for 3,855 yards, while Early and Haynes caught 159 passes between them. The defense, meanwhile, was led by three Pro-Bowlers: linebacker Renaldo Turnbull, cornerback Eric Allen, and defensive end Wayne Martin.

Linebacker Mark Fields was a feared tackler (pages 26-27).

Safety Sammy Knight finished the season with 75 tackles and six interceptions.

In 1995, the Saints got off to a disappointing start, losing their first five games before rebounding to finish 7–9. Any promise the Saints had shown evaporated in 1996, however, and Jim Mora resigned early into the 3–13 season. Mora, the Saints' all-time winningest coach, was replaced by interim coach Rick Venturi. New Orleans' fortunes were not changed by the coaching shuffle, though, and 1997 called for a major overhaul of the franchise.

This overhaul came in the hiring of Mike Ditka, the fiery former Chicago Bears coach. Ditka knew all about success in the NFL, having experienced Super Bowl wins as a head coach, assistant coach, and player. He accepted the Saints' coaching position after spending four years as a television football analyst. "I think we have the players to win our divi-

Speedy wideout Eddie Kennison.

sion," he said confidently. "That's our goal this year. We'll find a way to win."

The Saints made changes in their lineup as well. Jim Everett and Michael Haynes departed and were replaced by a new core of offensive players—quarterbacks Heath Shuler and Billy Joe Hobert, receivers Randal Hill and Andre Hastings, and running back Ray Zellars. On defense, rookie safety Sammy Knight emerged as a force in the secondary.

Swift receiver Keith Poole averaged an amazing 19 yards per catch.

The 1997 Saints doubled their win total of the previous season, finishing 6–10 and boasting one of the best defenses in the NFL. Unfortunately, their rebuilt offense finished dead last among the league's 30 teams.

1998 brought more new faces to New Orleans, including ball-hawking cornerback Tyronne Drakeford and receiver Sean Dawkins. The added personnel would not be enough, though. Shuler connected with Dawkins for 823 yards through the air, but the Saints' running attack was weak.

The defense fared no better. Despite the efforts of such standouts as Knight, linebacker Mark Fields, and tackle La'Roi Glover, New Orleans' defense fell from fourth-best in the league to one of the worst as the Saints finished 6–10.

THE RICKY WILLIAMS ERA

April 17, 1999, may go down as one of the most important dates in the history of the New Orleans Saints franchise. On that day, coach Mike Ditka traded away a total of eight draft picks in exchange for the fifth pick in that year's NFL draft. With the pick, the Saints chose running back Ricky Williams out of the University of Texas.

Tackle William Roaf dominated the line of scrimmage.

Star halfback Ricky Williams.

Saints fans hoped that head coach Jim Haslett would build New Orleans a winner at last.

In his college career, Williams had set a new NCAA Division I record for rushing yards. As a senior, he rushed for 2,124 yards and 27 touchdowns, capturing the Heisman Trophy. The 5-foot-10 and 225-pound Williams was described in one draft scouting report as "a workhorse runner with the movement of a racehorse and the durability of a plowhorse."

Coach Ditka was elated to acquire what he considered the central piece of the Saints' championship puzzle. Williams was just as excited and promised to prove his worth. "I don't have any goals as far as numbers go," the rookie said. "I want to go out and help Coach Ditka justify trading a whole draft for me. I want to get to the playoffs."

Unfortunately, the playoffs were but a dream in 1999 for the Saints, who finished 3–13. Williams struggled with injuries, and the offense sputtered under the guidance of two quarterbacks named Billy Joe—Hobert and Tolliver.

By the end of the season, Saints owner Tom Benson had seen enough. Head coach Mike Ditka was fired and replaced by Jim Haslett, the former defensive coordinator of the Pittsburgh Steelers. "[Haslett is] an energetic, tireless worker who has a passion for the game," explained Saints general manager Randy Mueller.

It remains to be seen if the Williams gamble will pay off, but the addition of such new talents as quarterback Jeff Blake and defensive tackle Norman Hand should only move the team upward. When the Saints do finally bring home the big trophy, there will undoubtedly be a big party in New Orleans, a city that really knows how to celebrate.